Cocktail Hour

Cocktail Hour

AUTHENTIC RECIPES

AND ILLUSTRATIONS

FROM 1920 TO 1960

SUSAN WAGGONER
AND ROBERT MARKEL

STEWART, TABORI & CHANG
NEW YORK

Published in 2006 by
Stewart, Tabori & Chang
115 West 18th Street
New York, NY 10011
www.abramsbooks.com

Library of Congress Cataloging-in-Publication Data

Waggoner, Susan.
  Cocktail hour : authentic recipes and illustrations from
1920 to 1960 / Susan Waggoner and Robert Markel.
     p. cm.
  Includes index.
  ISBN 1-58479-490-9
  1. Cocktails. I. Markel, Robert. II. Title.

TX951.W259 2006
641.8'74--dc22

2005020137

Edited by Dervla Kelly-Kohnen
Production by Jane Searle
Designed by Kay Schuckhart/Blond on Pond

The text of this book was composed in Adobe Garamond
Printed in Singapore

10 9 8 7 6 5 4 3 2 1

First Printing

Stewart, Tabori & Chang is a subsidiary of

LA MARTINIÈRE GROUPE

CONTENTS

Jargal

Introduction

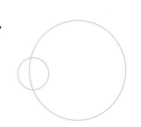

The cocktail hour — is there anything better to revive flagging workday spirits and reinvigorate one's overall belief in civilization? We think not.

We aren't, of course, talking about wild excess or the all-you-can-swallow tackiness of certain modern happy hours. Rather, we hark back to the days of the crisp linen napkin and silver shaker, when a single cocktail — well chosen, reverently mixed, and sipped against the backdrop of a twinkling skyline — was sufficient to banish the cares of the world.

The practice of serving early-evening cocktails was a natural outgrowth of the custom of late-afternoon tea. After the upheaval of World War I, going home to munch finger sandwiches and jam biscuits seemed far

too tame. A generation of youth had purchased freedom and independence at a high price, and they weren't about to surrender it. It was time for fun, and a decade-long party was just getting under way. In Europe and America, young women jettisoned their corsets, bobbed their hair, and scandalized their elders by wearing flesh-colored stockings with shockingly short dresses. Soon even proper young ladies were ordering drinks like the Hanky Panky, the Maiden's Blush, and the Goldfish, and Prohibition couldn't dampen their spirits.

The glamour of the cocktail hour waned for ordinary folks during the Depression, although it continued to be luminously celebrated on the silver screen. World War II took its own toll, as most people were too busy or too preoccupied to indulge in an hour's quiet relaxation. The

custom came back full force in the flush 1950s and lasted into the 1960s. Many's a baby boomer who can remember the long wait for dinner as Mom and Dad drank gin and tonics on the patio. And when it became known that the youthful new president, John Kennedy, was a daiquiri man, the drink became an overnight sensation. By the late 1960s and early 1970s, when protest marches, granola, and body painting were in fashion, the cocktail hour seemed a quaint curio of the past. It was only in hiding, though, momentarily camouflaged as the predinner wine and cheese event, a kind of cocktail hour without the cocktails.

Today, we're glad to say, the cocktail hour is jubilantly ascendant, with cocktails more splendid and plentiful than ever. Don't you think it's time we brushed up our mixology skills, added some recipes to our repertoire, and toasted this noble tradition?

HERE'S HOW

Mixing a good cocktail is not tremendously difficult, so long as you are willing to take a bit of time and pay attention to what you are doing. Which, we know, is harder than it sounds — hence the shortage of really good mixologists. Here are some simple principles to keep in mind:

Follow directions. The order of adding ingredients, the instructions to shake rather than stir, measurements, and other parts of the recipe are there for a reason. Adhere to them.

Use the best ingredients you can afford. Poor-quality liquor does not taste better when combined with mixers, juices, bitters, or other ingredients. It is better to stock the ingredients for a few good cocktails than for a hundred poor ones.

Have ingredients and equipment ready. Once you start mixing a drink, you should be able to finish it without pausing. If you shake and strain your cocktail into the waiting glass, then have to pause to cut or search for a garnish, the spirits will begin to separate and warm. This is not a happy situation, and one a good bartender will avoid.

Live in the ice age. The key ingredient in a good cocktail isn't alcohol — it's cold. Make sure glasses, mixers, and juices are well chilled, and that you have a plentiful amount of ice on hand.

Don't make too many drinks at once. A cocktail is meant to be drunk as soon as it is made. Mixing a pitcher of martinis may sound good, but unless there are enough drinkers to consume the entire pitcher in one pouring, resist the temptation.

Be vigilant. The last drink you mix should taste as good as the first. Don't get sloppy. If you don't have duplicate sets of equipment, wash, rinse, and dry shakers, shot glasses, measuring spoons, and other equipment between drinks.

MEASURE UP

When it comes to mixing a perfect cocktail, the small volume of a single finished drink makes accurate measurement extremely important. Early cocktail books often used bar terminology, calling for measurements such as a shot, a pony, a wineglass, or a bar glass. The problem was that, while a shot is usually $1\frac{1}{2}$ ounces and a pony is generally 1 ounce, this is not always the case, and the variation among glasses could be great. Most modern mixology books call for standardized measures such as ounces and tablespoons, a format we have followed in this book.

Recipes can be easily doubled or tripled to serve more than one guest at a time. Do not, however, mix more cocktails than will be drunk immediately. Cocktails do not keep well, and the best drinks are always the freshest. You can multiply a recipe to make as many drinks as needed; just take care to keep the proportions true to the original. Here are some measurements to help you.

- 1 dash = 4 or 5 drops
- 1 standard shot or jigger = 1 ½ ounces
- 1 pony = 1 ounce
- 4 tablespoons = ¼ cup
- 3 tablespoons = 1 ½ ounces
- 1 cup = 8 ounces
- 1 tablespoon = ½ ounce
- 1 tablespoon = 3 teaspoons

And to convert to or from metric:

- 1 gill = 5 ounces
- ⅜ gill = 1 ½ ounces
- 5 milliliters = 1 teaspoon
- 15 milliliters = 1 tablespoon
- 29.57 milliliters = 1 ounce
- 44.355 milliliters = 1 ½ ounces

THE PERFECT COCKTAIL PARTY

Prohibition wasn't all bad — thanks to it, we have the delightful institution known as the cocktail party. When the Volstead Act took effect on that cold January night in 1920, many Americans weren't prepared to forgo their favorite spirits. And, as time went on, their numbers grew. By 1925, New York City on its own boasted

at least thirty thousand — and possibly as many as a hundred thousand — speakeasies. Naturally, not everybody chose to flout the law in a hideaway that could be raided by the police at any moment. To fill the need, the at-home cocktail party was born.

Usually held in the early evening, the cocktail party was a purposely effervescent affair, smoothing out the wrinkles of the day just past and casting a golden glow on the evening ahead. No serious salon, the cocktail party promoted playful conversation and a general air of relaxation. Soon it became customary to serve drinks with an array of light snacks to fill the gap until dinner. Cocktail dresses — dressier than daytime wear but less formal than full evening regalia — began appearing in the 1920s, and men's fashions followed suit with what eventually became the sports jacket.

Had the "noble experiment" of enforced national temperance ended after a few misguided years, the cocktail party might have faded into oblivion. But Prohibition remained in force until December 1933, by which time the cocktail party had become an established fact of life. Girls who had been flickering flappers when it began were now sophisticated ladies in their thirties with a full cocktail wardrobe begging to be worn. The crowd that had been young and single in 1920 was mar-

BITTER
CAMPARI

a theme — such as retro glamour, tiki mania, stand-out hors d'oeuvres, or a menu of adventurous new cocktails? Homing in on a few focal points will help you make food and beverage choices, and can help your guests get in the spirit as well. When Frank Sinatra threw cocktail parties during the Rat Pack days, his invitations specified "Black Tie and Sunglasses." Film star Marion Davies's guests were greeted with a vision of cocktail shakers lined up beside the pool.

 Set the day and time. One of the most wonderful things about a cocktail party is that you decide when it ends, and it's customary to specify not only the date but the hours on the invitation. Traditionally, cocktail parties last from 6 until 8 in the evening — after the workday is finished and early enough for people to go on to dinner. Weekend afternoon cocktail parties can be earlier, since the workday does not interfere.

Set the drink menu. Don't rush out and buy ingredients for every conceivable cocktail under the sun. Not only is this an expensive plan, but you may well end up with a lot of mismatched ingredients that will never be used. You probably already know what cocktails are popular with your friends these days, as well as the quirky tastes of a few. Start

ried by 1934, with homes and apartments equipped with liquor cabinets, ice buckets, glasses, and an assortment of barware worthy of the Ritz. The cocktail party had become a way of life, and it slipped into the post-Prohibition mainstream without losing a step.

To all of which we give three hearty cheers. Few social encounters are as pleasantly civilized as a well-run cocktail party. Those of you who haven't given one are missing one of the great pleasures of socializing. If you're a novice, or need to touch up your party-giving skills, here are a few tips to keep in mind.

 Make it special. What will make your party memorable? Are you going to have

with this, and widen your menu to make a few other choices as well. You can calculate how much liquor to get by estimating that, over a two- to three-hour cocktail party, each guest will consume about three drinks. While you're calculating the spirits needed, don't forget to calculate the types and amounts of mixers, fruit juices, lemons, limes, oranges, and garnishes that go in the drinks as well. When setting your drink menu, don't forget that some of your guests will probably not be drinking alcohol. You'll be a big hit as a host if you provide a few special drinks for them as well, instead of just ordinary soda.

Set the food menu.

Because cocktail parties are between-meal events, people expect to be offered an array of light snacks. They don't need to be elaborate or expensive, but they should be easy to eat, and they should "hold" well — that is, they shouldn't become unappealing or inedible if they aren't eaten within the first five minutes. Variety is important, and you should offer enough different types of snacks so that everyone will find something to nibble on, regardless of their tastes or dietary preferences. You don't need to spend the day of your party making fussy finger food, either. There's nothing wrong with setting out spreads, crackers, party breads, and other fixings and letting guests assemble their own snacks. In fact, it's often a great ice-breaking strategy because it gives guests something to do.

Take inventory of supplies for your guests.

How many guests will there be? For each person, you will need:

3 drinks
5 hors d'oeuvres
1 pound ice

3 glasses

3 napkins

Any plates and forks needed for
hors d'oeuvres

 Take inventory of bar equipment.
Essentials include an ice bucket, cocktail
shaker and strainer, measuring glasses,
measuring spoons, stirring spoons,
swizzle sticks, toothpicks, zester,
cutting board, paring knife, and waste
receptacle. If you are going to be
making drinks that need to be shaken,
it's wonderful to have more than one
shaker to work with.

 Be prepared. On the day of the event,
do a last-minute check on all supplies.
Make sure to refrigerate your mixers and
juices well in advance, to allow them to
get really cold. Cocktail garnishes can be
prepared ahead of time and kept,
covered, in the refrigerator until guests
begin to arrive. Most cocktail parties set
the mood with background music —
have fun picking out a selection of music
and place CDs within easy reach.
Finally, survey the room from your
guests' point of view. Is the furniture
arranged to facilitate mingling and easy
conversation? Are there chairs for guests
who may want to sit down? Are there
places to set drinks and hors d'oeuvres,
and receptacles for used napkins, olive
pits, and other debris?

 Finally, have fun. Remember, it's up to
you to have a good time too — nothing
can dampen spirits faster than a host or
hostess who is grimly and obviously "on
duty." Maybe you did put out the
wrong set of napkins, or maybe your
friend from work could use another hors
d'oeuvres or two. But once the party
starts, relax and take a bit of a laissez -
faire attitude. No one will remember
which napkins you used, and your friend
is perfectly capable of helping herself.

12 Vintage Classics

Everyone should know to make these classic cocktails. For their histories, variations, and further details, please see our books *Vintage Cocktails* and *Cocktails A-Go-Go*.

STIR IN A MIXING GLASS AND STRAIN INTO A CHILLED COCKTAIL GLASS

Martini: 1 ½ oz. gin, 1 tbsp. (or less) dry vermouth; garnish with an olive. A vodka Martini, on the other hand, should be shaken.

Tequila Sunrise: 1 ½ oz. tequila, 3 oz. orange juice; after straining into a cocktail glass, add ¾ oz. grenadine; garnish with a slice of lime.

SHAKE WITH CRACKED ICE AND STRAIN INTO A CHILLED COCKTAIL GLASS

Daiquiri: 1 ½ oz. white rum, 1 tsp. sugar, juice of 1 ½ small limes.

Mai Tai: 1 oz. light rum, 1 oz. dark rum, ½ oz. orange curaçao, 1 ½ tsp. simple syrup, 1 ½ tsp. orgeat (almond) syrup; garnish with a lime peel and a mint sprig.

Manhattan: 1 ½ oz. rye, ¾ oz. sweet vermouth, 2 dashes Angostura bitters; garnish with a maraschino cherry.

Margarita: 1 ½ oz. tequila, ½ oz. orange liqueur, juice of 1 large lime. Prepare glass by rubbing rim with a wedge of lime, then dipping in salt.

IN THE ORDER GIVEN, POUR INTO A GLASS WITH ICE AND STIR

Bloody Mary: 3 oz. tomato juice, juice of ½ lemon, 1 ½ oz. vodka, 2 dashes Worcestershire sauce, dash of black pepper, dash of Tabasco sauce (optional); garnish with a celery stalk.

Gimlet: 1 ½ oz. gin, ½ oz. Rose's lime juice, lime wedge (in the glass, not as a garnish).

Gin and Tonic: 1 ½ oz. gin, tonic water; garnish with a lime wedge. Prepare glass by rubbing rim with a wedge of lime.

Highball: 1 ½ oz. liquor, 3oz. mixer. Popular combinations include scotch and soda, rum and coke, and bourbon and ginger ale.

Screwdriver: 2 oz. vodka, 3 oz. orange juice; garnish with a slice of orange.

Tom Collins: 1 tsp. sugar, juice of 1 lemon, 1 ½ oz. gin, 4–5 oz. club soda.

THE MOST IMPORTANT INGREDIENT: COLD

So why didn't the lords and ladies of the past drink cocktails? There were wassail bowls and celebratory cups aplenty. Why didn't William the Conqueror toast his triumph with a gin and tonic? Why didn't the adventurous Marco Polo find Chinese emperors sipping slings and Martinis? Probably because the most important ingredient in any good cocktail — *cold* — was missing. While wine and straight liquor are palatable at room temperature, an unchilled cocktail does not taste nearly as good as its components taste on their own. Before ice was commercially harvested, only the wealthiest could afford it. In America, plantation owners displayed their affluence by treating guests to ice cream and mint juleps, luxuries that demanded extravagant amounts of ice. Commercial harvesting began in the mid-nineteenth century, and as transport and methods of insulation improved, ice became available to the masses for the first time in history. Soon the modern cocktail, chilled to icy perfection, was all the rage.

Alexander the Great

Once upon a time there was a drink called the Alexander (see page 18). Then, according to Lucius Beebe in *The Stork Club Bar Book*, Nelson Eddy came along and whipped up this improvement. For you youngsters out there — no, Nelson Eddy wasn't an early-model sedan. In the 1930s, he teamed with Jeanette MacDonald (best remembered for singing "San Francisco" opposite Clark Gable while the city fell down around her) to make the kind of operatic musicals that against all odds made a world teetering toward war seem quaint, old-fashioned, and relatively safe. We're delighted that, in addition to playing dashing Royal Canadian Mounties, sea captains, West Point cadets, and Russian princes, Eddy was also a fair mixologist. We like to drink this one on Valentine's Day, when something rich with a hint of chocolate is called for, and when our beloved won't mind if we hum along with Nelson and Jeanette.

1 ½ oz. vodka

½ oz. crème de cacao

½ oz. coffee liqueur

½ oz. cream

Combine ingredients in a cocktail shaker with cracked ice and, as *The Stork Club Bar Book* directs, "shake until cold as Siberia." Strain into a chilled cocktail glass. We also pass along the book's admonition to "watch your Steppes," as too many of these smooth and sweet cocktails can stimulate a ravenous appetite.

FOR YOUR FURTHER DRINKING PLEASURE: An Alexander the Great made without the addition of coffee liqueur appears from time to time in vintage drink books as the **Barbara** cocktail, and is one of the earliest examples of a vodka drink served in America. As noted above, Alexander the Great is a variation of an already existing cocktail, the **Alexander**. The Alexander is made in the same fashion but with gin instead of vodka, and without the addition of coffee liqueur. For the gin Alexander, increase the crème de cacao to ¾ ounce. And, of course, there's the most famous drink in this family, the **Brandy Alexander**. Make it with 1 ½ ounces brandy, ½ ounce crème de cacao, and 1 ounce cream. Delicious!

Algonquin

*I must say we behaved extremely badly . . .
Gertrude Stein did us the most harm when she said,
"You're all a lost generation." That got around to
certain people and we all said, Whee! We're lost.*

— Dorothy Parker, 1956

Known irreverently as "the Gonk" by the writers, artists, and all-around smarty pants who formed the hotel's infamous Round Table, the venerable Algonquin Hotel refuses to take credit for this appealing cocktail. Chances are it was invented one *après déjeuner*, in quarters inhabited by a Round Table member. The fact that the hotel itself honored Prohibition hardly mattered to the group, who weren't about to be deterred by anything as ephemeral as a ban on liquor. A few of these on a long, lazy afternoon will make anyone feel witty.

If you don't have rye on hand, another type of whiskey will give a fair approximation of the drink. For the real thing, however, rye is the spirit of choice.

2 oz. rye

1 oz. dry vermouth

1 oz. pineapple juice

Combine ingredients in a cocktail shaker with cracked ice. Shake briskly and strain into a chilled cocktail glass. Contemporary mixologists almost invariably garnish this with cubes of pineapple. Although pineapple is delicious, the original garnish was a maraschino cherry.

IT STARTED WITH A JOKE

One afternoon in 1919, a group of journalists gathered for lunch to welcome one of their number, Alexander Woollcott, back from duty as a war correspondent. The welcome turned to a roast, and so much fun was had by all — including the roastee — that the group reconvened for lunch the next day . . . and the next . . . and the one after that. For the next ten years, the group known to the public as the Algonquin Round Table (and to themselves as the Vicious Circle) would meet daily in a showdown of barbed wit. Or so the legend goes. In reality, few members of the group had the leisure or the cash to swan away endless afternoons in a hotel dining room. In 1956, Dorothy Parker told an interviewer, "I wasn't there often — it cost too much." Nevertheless, Parker and her compatriots — a list that included Robert Sherwood, George Kaufman, Robert Benchley, Franklin P. Adams, Edna Ferber, Heywood Broun, Noel Coward, Harpo Marx, and Tallulah Bankhead — showed up often enough to make a permanent name for themselves. By the end of the 1920s, the Round Table had become a noted tourist attraction, and members felt more like zoo animals than a table of friends. The Crash of 1929 dealt a final blow, with many of the wits — including Benchley, Kaufman, and Parker — forced to seek work in that dreaded sinkhole of the far west, Hollywood.

Bee's Kiss

It's a fair bet that any drink with the name "bee" in the title is bound to incorporate a drizzle of honey. In the case of this pre-Prohibition cocktail, the name has a flirtatious meaning as well: A "bee's kiss" was the term for fluttering the eyelashes against the cheeks, lips, or nose of one's beloved.

2 oz. gold rum (or two thirds gold and one third dark rum)
1 oz. cream
2 tsp. honey

Place ingredients in a cocktail shaker with cracked ice. Shake and strain into a chilled cocktail glass. If desired, dust with a sprinkle of ginger or nutmeg.

FOR YOUR FURTHER DRINKING PLEASURE: Replace the cream with the juice of 1 lime, omit the sprinkle of spice, and you have a delightful cocktail called an **Air Mail** — which must have seemed quite the thing back in 1920s, when instrumentation was lacking and pilots flew by instructions that said, "Follow the tracks of the Long Island Railroad past Belmont Park race track, keeping Jamaica on the left. Cross New York over the lower end of Central Park."

Blue Train Special

This cocktail first appeared in the 1920s, well before the opulent restaurant in the Gare de Lyon or the train that plies the South African veld. We can only assume, then, that this cocktail is associated with Le Train Bleu, the French railway that ran from the Côte d'Azur to Paris and Calais. In its day, Le Train Bleu was the swiftest, most luxurious way to cross France, and it isn't too hard to picture Ernest Hemingway, Coco Chanel, or Gary Cooper — frequent passengers all — sipping cocktails as the scenery spooled by.

1 ½ oz. brandy
1 ½ oz. chilled pineapple juice
3 oz. ice cold champagne

Pour brandy and pineapple juice into a cocktail shaker with cracked ice. Shake and strain into a chilled champagne flute or wineglass. Immediately top with champagne.

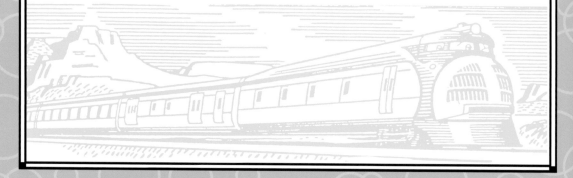

Bobby Burns

The Savoy Cocktail Book describes this as "One of the very best Whiskey Cocktails," and notes that it's a sure seller on Saint Andrew's Day. We concur, and rarely let a November 30th slip by without one. Or, for that matter, a January 25 — the birthday of the poet for whom the drink was named, and a good reason to raise a glass to all things Scottish.

¾ oz. scotch
¾ oz. sweet vermouth
3 dashes Benedictine

Combine ingredients in a cocktail shaker with cracked ice. Shake and strain into a chilled cocktail glass. Squeeze a piece of lemon peel over the top but do not garnish.

Bronx

If ew drinks have ever taken a town by storm the way the Bronx took New York at the turn of the century. Today, there are almost as many conflicting stories about its origins as there are versions of the drink itself. One of the most convincing claims is documented in *The Old Waldorf-Astoria Bar Book*, published in 1935. The book awards the honor to Johnnie Solon, a well-known bartender at the old Waldorf. As Solon told the story, he was making a Duplex, a popular drink of the day, when the headwaiter from the hotel's main dining room challenged him to invent a new cocktail, saying a customer had bet he could not do so. Solon quickly mixed a libation and handed it to Traverson, the headwaiter, to try. "By God! You've really got something new here," Traverson exclaimed. "Have you got plenty of oranges? If you haven't, you better stock up, because I am going to sell a lot of these cocktails during lunch." Traverson's instincts were spot on, and it wasn't long until the bar was ordering several cases of oranges a day to meet the demand. As for the cocktail's name, Solon explained that the day before he had visited the Bronx Zoo and seen many strange new beasts whose names he did not know. Just before Traverson carried the experimental cocktail to the customer, he asked Solon what to call the drink. Thinking of the strange new beasts at the zoo, Solon decided to call the new cocktail a Bronx.

> *The gay dogs of the Murray Hill age drank it . . . It had the same cachet that Maxim's had, or Delmonico's . . .*
>
> — The Hour,
> Bernard DeVoto

Bronx
(Original)

2 oz. gin

1 oz. orange juice

Dash of dry vermouth

Dash of sweet vermouth

Combine ingredients in a shaker with cracked ice. Shake and strain into a chilled cocktail glass.

FOR YOUR FURTHER DRINKING PLEASURE: Close kin to the Bronx is the **Montauk**, made by combining 1 ounce each of gin, dry vermouth, and sweet vermouth with a dash of Peychaud bitters. The gin-vermouth combination was popular on both sides of the Atlantic. At the bar of London's Savoy Hotel one could order a **Midnight**, which had the same gin-vermouth ratios as the Montauk but used 1 tablespoon orange juice and a dash of absinthe in place of bitters. The same cocktail can still be enjoyed today with Pernod or Absente giving a fair approximation of the outlawed absinthe. Close kin to the Midnight was the **Queen's Cocktail**, which began by smashing a slice of orange and a slice of pineapple together in a cocktail shaker, then adding 1 ounce each of gin, dry vermouth, and sweet vermouth, shaking with ice and straining into a chilled cocktail glass.

BRONX II

2 oz. gin
1 oz. dry vermouth
1 oz. sweet vermouth

Combine ingredients in a cocktail shaker with cracked ice. Shake and strain into a chilled cocktail glass. Squeeze a piece of orange peel over the top.

FOR YOUR FURTHER DRINKING PLEASURE: This version of the Bronx, with the addition of the juice from a quarter of an orange and a dash of Pernod, was known as a **Minnehaha**. One of our favorite bits of nonsense appears in Robert Vermeire's otherwise sound book, *Cocktails: How To Mix Them,* written in 1922. After describing the drink, he asserts that, "In China this cocktail is known as the Minnehaha Cocktail . . . Minnehaha is the Chinese for 'Laughing Water.'" Vermeire was 6,300 miles and several cultures off: *Minnehaha* does indeed mean laughing water, but the word is Native American, and known to most people through its appearance in Longfellow's epic poem *The Song of Hiawatha.*

BRONX III

2 oz. gin
1 oz. dry vermouth
1 tbsp. orange juice

Combine ingredients in a cocktail shaker with cracked ice. Shake and strain into a chilled cocktail glass.

FOR YOUR FURTHER DRINKING PLEASURE: From Harry's Bar in Paris comes the **Bulldog**. To mix, increase the orange juice to 1 ounce, place it with ice and gin in a highball glass, then fill to the top with ginger ale and stir.

Brown Derby

People have to drink somewhere. Why not here?

— Joan Crawford as *Mildred Pierce*, 1945

DINE *and* DANCE

With its distinctive shape and star-studded tables, the Brown Derby was *the* place to see and be seen in glamorous old Hollywood. Conceived by Cecile B. DeMille, it opened in 1929 and, after a short stint as Willard's Chicken Inn, acquired the name that made it famous. Even if you never visited the Derby, chances are you've seen at least a bit of it — the oval bar from the original Derby was used in the movie *Mildred Pierce*. As for the distinctive bowler shape of the place, it was more than just a gimmick — water pumped to the top trickled continuously down the sides into a moat, providing customers with an early form of air-conditioning. Ironically, the drink that bears its name wasn't invented at the Derby but at another Hollywood haunt, the Vendome Club — which seems to us a pretty high compliment.

THE BROWN DERBY RESTAURANT — 1628 N. VINE ST. — HOLLYWOOD, CALIF.

2 oz. whiskey

1 oz. grapefruit juice

1 – 2 tbsp. honey, depending on your sweet tooth

Combine ingredients in a cocktail shaker with cracked ice. Shake vigorously and strain into a chilled cocktail glass.

FOR YOUR FURTHER DRINKING PLEASURE: While researching this book, we persistently came across another version of the Brown Derby whose origins we could not discover but which, at least during the mid-1950s, was as well known as the original. To make it, follow the directions and proportions above, substituting dark rum for the whiskey, lime juice for grapefruit, and maple syrup for the honey.

Clover Club

Not to be outdone by the smarty pants of the Algonquin Round Table in New York, Philadelphia's Bellevue Hotel hosted its own group of convivial wits, wags, and all-around bon vivants. They convened regularly in the heady days before Prohibition cast its shadow over the land, and to them we owe the Clover Club cocktail. Though nearly forgotten today, the cocktail was the Cosmopolitan or Bloody Mary of its day, so famous that a song of the same name appeared in 1918 and so popular that it ranked sixth on a favorite cocktails list in 1934. We're not quite sure why the Clover Club lost favor almost overnight. Perhaps it was sped on its way to oblivion by bartenders' penchant for replacing the raspberry syrup originally called for with grenadine, or maybe the harsh and poisonous bathtub gin of Prohibition left people jaded to the charms of the juniper berry. We think it's time for a revival of the Clover Club as originally served, and if you go to the trouble to mix it with high-quality gin, you will be well rewarded for your efforts.

If the notion of a drink with raw egg white makes you hesitate, you may leave it out. It was, however, a frequent ingredient in early-twentieth-century drinks and adds smoothness to the drink without over burdening the delicate gin.

1 ½ oz. gin
1 tablespoon raspberry syrup
1 egg white, or egg white substitute equivalent to white from one egg
Juice of one lime, freshly squeezed and strained of seeds

Place ingredients in a cocktail shaker with cracked ice. Shake gently and strain into a chilled cocktail glass.

FOR YOUR FURTHER DRINKING PLEASURE: If you are lucky enough to have fresh mint on hand, crush a sprig lightly and add it to the shaker, being sure to strain it out when the cocktail is poured. This variation, known as a **Clover Leaf**, is immensely refreshing on a hot summer day. Another variation of this drink is the aptly named **Gloom Lifter**. To make one, follow the recipe and method above, substituting whiskey for gin, the juice of ½ lemon in place of lime juice, and adding a dash of brandy.

Corpse Reviver

To be taken at 11 A.M., or whenever steam and energy are needed.

— The Savoy Cocktail Book, 1930

We love this one for its delightfully macabre name and the mental image that leaps to mind. In the early years of cocktailmania, there were dozens of recipes for Corpse Revivers, some of which seemed to us likely to achieve the opposite effect, guaranteeing an early and untimely demise, and some of which called for such an extended list of ingredients one might slip away into oblivion before assembling them all. This was one of the best we sampled, and refreshingly simple to make.

1 ½ oz. brandy
¾ oz. calvados
¾ oz. sweet vermouth

Combine ingredients in a mixing glass with ice. Stir well and strain into a chilled cocktail glass.

FOR YOUR FURTHER DRINKING PLEASURE: If you replace the sweet vermouth with a like amount of orange liqueur, add a dash of freshly squeezed lemon juice, shake with ice, and strain into a chilled glass, you have the **Deauville**, named for that glamorous old diva of a resort town in the heart of Calvados country. Also worth noting is the World War I–era **Depth Bomb**, not to be confused with the **Depth Charge**, which is a half-and-half mix of gin and blonde Lillet with a dash of Pernod. **The Depth Bomb**, on the other hand, is half brandy and half Calvados, with several dashes of grenadine and one of freshly squeezed lemon juice, shaken with ice and strained into a chilled glass.

Douglas Fairbanks

It all started with a hunting lodge in the hills — Beverly Hills — that Douglas Fairbanks bought as a wedding present for his bride, Mary Pickford, in 1919. The hills were ramshackle wilderness, the population of the entire city less than seven hundred. That began to change when Fairbanks and Pickford transformed the lodge into a twenty-two room mansion attached to twenty acres of lagoons, riding trails, stables, tennis courts, and a private swimming pool — Hollywood's first — big enough to go canoeing on. Pickfair became the most famous home in America, site of carefree frolics that created the image of a fast, fun, glittering town devoted to making illusion reality.

Soon tourists were flocking to see the equally opulent mansions flung up by other stars. Fresh-faced girls in Iowa practiced walking and talking like Tallulah, Bette, and Joan. And everybody — absolutely everybody — enjoyed ordering cocktails named after legendary stars.

According to many biographical accounts, it was Pickford, not Fairbanks, who was the more enthusiastic drinker at Pickfair. Nevertheless, a cocktail bearing the name of the man who first played Zorro, Robin Hood, and Don Juan on the silver screen has been passed down to us. It must have made a lovely ornament for the eighteen-foot antique mahogany bar Pickford bestowed upon him one Christmas.

1 ½ oz. gin

1 ½ oz. dry vermouth

Pour ingredients into a mixing glass over ice. Stir briskly and strain into a chilled cocktail glass. Garnish with a twist of lemon and a twist of orange.

FOR YOUR FURTHER DRINKING PLEASURE: This drink very closely resembles the proportions of the 1880s-era original Martini. And, like the Martini, later variations reduce the ratio of vermouth substantially, calling for 2 ounces gin to 1 ounce vermouth. Other recipes we've seen call for the addition of a few drops of grenadine, and the most exotic call for 1 ½ ounces gin to ¾ ounce each of vermouth and apricot brandy.

El Floridita

There was a time when all roads led to Havana. From America, you had your choice of conveyances — a leisurely cruise ship, a ferry that would transport your vehicle as well as your luggage, or a special flight that left at sunset, entertained you with dinner and an onboard pianist, deposited you for an evening's revelry, then served you breakfast on the way back to Miami. One of Havana's top draws was El Floridita, proclaimed one of the world's seven best bars by *Esquire* in 1953. Frequent visitors to the place included the Duke and Duchess of Windsor, Gary Cooper, Ava Gardner, Errol Flynn, Spencer Tracy, Rocky Marciano, and a whole floating contingent of bullfighters, writers, and artists. To satisfy their world-weary tastes, the owner and bartender Constantino Ribalaigua created any number of inspired drinks, including a spectacular house special and a version of the daiquiri that still shimmers today.

The cocktail that bears the Floridita name requires some skill to mix. Be wary of adding too much crème de cacao and grenadine. Neither of these should overwhelm the drink. Rather, they're there to provide a finishing hint of sweetness.

1 ½ oz. white rum

1 tbsp. sweet vermouth

Juice of ½ lime, strained

Dash of white crème de cacao

Dash of grenadine

Pour ingredients into a cocktail shaker over cracked ice. Shake briskly and strain into a chilled cocktail glass. Garnish with a twist of lime.

FOR YOUR FURTHER DRINKING PLEASURE: Nothing lasts forever. Except, perhaps, for El Floridita, which we're told still lights up the Havana evenings. When Castro came to power in the late 1950s, a new drink was born, the **Mulata**. To make one, follow the recipe above but omit the sweet vermouth and grenadine.

Combine the rum, lime juice, and crème de cacao with ice in a blender, whir until a snowlike slush is achieved, and pour into a frosted cocktail glass. Purportedly, this drink got its name from its color — a shade of green that reminded imbibers of the olive drab worn by the new regime. To be honest, this explanation never made complete sense to us. A little research leads to another and perhaps more likely explanation: When Bacardi fled Cuba during the revolution, cocktails had to be mixed with a different brand of local rum, Ron Mulata.

Embassy

Just as New York's 21 Club offered sanctuary to well-heeled Easterners during Prohibition, so too did the Embassy Club flourish on the West Coast. The speakeasy par excellence, located on Hollywood Boulevard, catered almost exclusively to the stars of the day. No wonder they felt at home there — the interiors were done by the set designer who later did Rick's American Café and other backdrops for *Casablanca*. The Embassy gave the world several memorable cocktails, the most famous of which is probably Satan's Whiskers (page 79). We think this one, which bears the club's name, is also worth reviving. We commend it for redirecting spirits most commonly found in hot Yuletide grogs to the ice cold precincts of the cocktail shaker.

¾ oz. brandy
¾ oz. Cointreau
¾ oz. Jamaican rum
Juice of 1 lime, strained
Dash of Angostura bitters

Combine ingredients in a cocktail shaker with cracked ice. Shake well, strain into a chilled cocktail glass, and garnish with a twist of lime.

Floridita Daiquiri

Once upon a time, when Havana was America's weekend playground, a bar called El Floridita ranked among the world's best — largely because its owner, Constantino Ribalaigua, was one of the world's greatest barmen. Creative, exacting, and passionate about his craft, he went to enormous lengths to produce outstanding cocktails. He pursued many recipes and variations in search of the perfect daiquiri, and finally had a special ice machine imported from America. The results were well worth his effort, and this stylized version of a frozen daiquiri deserves to be drunk with reverence and a sigh of deep appreciation.

1½ oz. white rum, preferably Bacardi

Juice of 1 lime, strained

5 drops maraschino liqueur

1 teaspoon sugar

Place ingredients in a blender with a scoopful of ice. Blend until smooth and pour at once into a chilled cocktail glass.

FOR YOUR FURTHER DRINKING PLEASURE: El Floridita's owner and master mixologist served this daiquiri frozen, but we're happy to report that it's just as delicious when the ingredients are shaken with ice, strained into a chilled cocktail glass, and garnished with a twist of lime. If you omit the maraschino liqueur from the Floridita Daiquiri, you will have a classic daiquiri, which the Havana watering hole called a **Daiquiri Naturel**. And if you pour the ingredients of a Daiquiri Naturel into a tall glass filled with ice, add 3 ounces club soda, stir with a swizzle stick and garnish with a slice of lime, you have the delightful **Ron Collins,** just the thing for a hot day in the tropics — or anywhere, for that matter.

Flying Fortress

It seemed only natural for this 1940s cocktail to take the name of one of the greatest heroes of World War II — the B-17 bomber, affectionately known as the Flying Fortress to the men whose lives depended on it. This drink is not for the faint of heart. Like the plane itself, if you run into more than one of these, you'll know it.

2 oz. cognac

1 oz. vodka

1 tbsp. Pernod or other anise liqueur

1 tbsp. orange liqueur

Juice of ¼ lime, strained

Place ingredients in a cocktail shaker with ice and shake well. Strain into a chilled cocktail glass and garnish with a twist of lemon peel. For a fancier presentation, rim the glass with orange liqueur, then dip in sugar. Depending on how far whimsy takes you, you can also cut the lemon peel in the shape of small propellers.

LIFE IN 1944

- Everything is Rosie: 3.5 million women work on assembly lines. America can produce a bomber in thirteen days, a cargo ship in seventeen.
- Paper shortages and shipping expenses cause publishers to try something new — paperback books.
- Canned fruit shortages make Jell-O a popular new home dessert.
- Debuting in grocery stores: Chiquita bananas.
- Debuting on Broadway: *Oklahoma!* The top ticket price is $3.
- Debuting on the radio: Roy Rogers and *The Adventures of Ozzie and Harriet*

Goldfish

Prohibition brought out the most amazing creativity in people. According to William Grimes's *Straight Up or On the Rocks*, a Park Avenue speakeasy called the Aquarium maintained its aura of swank by mixing bootleg gin with Goldwasser, a citrus-infused liqueur with flakes of gold swirling through it. The glitter put customers in a good mood and kept them from dwelling on the harsh taste of bad gin. Since a gigantic aquarium formed part of the bar, it made sense — in a screwball kind of way — to name the drink a Goldfish. We still enjoy it on New Year's Eve, when a glass of confetti seems perfect for the occasion.

1 oz. gin
1 oz. dry vermouth
1 oz. Goldwasser

Combine ingredients in an ice-filled mixing glass and stir well. Pour into a chilled cocktail glass, holding back the ice but taking care not to strain out the gold flakes.
FOR YOUR FURTHER DRINKING PLEASURE: Although we cannot prove it, we suspect that the Goldfish was a jazzed-up version of a humbler drink of the era, the **Gold**, which consists of 1 ½ ounces each of gin and sweet vermouth, stirred with ice and a dash of orange bitters and served in a chilled cocktail glass. There was also a beguiling little number called the **Futurity**, which used equal parts sloe gin and sweet vermouth, and Angostura rather than orange bitters.

Gloria Swanson Champagne Cocktail

Long before she played Norma Desmond in *Sunset Boulevard*, Gloria Swanson was the most sophisticated actress in Hollywood. According to Lucius Beebe, cocktail connoisseur and chronicler of New York café society, the glamorous actress simply adored starting her day with this stunningly chic cocktail. The recipe below is for a cocktail half the size reputedly quaffed by the actress — which is probably about as much as most of us can handle without looking a bit the worse for wear.

1 oz. cognac
8 oz. very dry, very cold champagne

Place two or three ice cubes in a tall collins glass. Pour cognac over ice, then add champagne. Stir and garnish with a twist of lemon peel.

FOR YOUR FURTHER DRINKING PLEASURE: Feeling a bit blah? Try a **Champagne Pick Me Up**, as served in the 1930s at the bar of the Ritz Hotel, Paris. Begin with cognac and ice in a tall glass, add 3 ounces chilled orange juice, and a dash of grenadine if desired, then fill to the top with champagne. A lighter version of this drink, the **Champagne Fizz**, is made by omitting the cognac and adding just 1 ounce orange juice, then filling with chilled champagne and garnishing with a twist of orange peel.

HOLLYWOOD LOVES CHAMPAGNE

There comes a time in every woman's life when the only thing that helps is a glass of champagne.

— Bette Davis in *Old Acquaintance*, 1943

Champagne is the symbol for glamour and romance, onscreen as well as off. Besides quaffing champagne cocktails at the Stork Club, Gloria Swanson, as the fading Norma Desmond, drank them throughout *Sunset Boulevard*. Marilyn Monroe dunked potato chips in champagne in *The Seven Year Itch*, and Audrey Hepburn and George Peppard drank it first thing in the morning in *Breakfast at Tiffany's*. Katharine Hepburn and Jimmy Stewart got high as kites on it in *The Philadelphia Story*, and in *Casablanca*, Humphrey Bogart drank liquor when he was alone, but with Ingrid Bergman his drink was always — and only — champagne.

Hanky Panky

Until the last few decades, mixologists of note were almost always men. One exception was Ada Coleman. Affectionately known as Coley, she became the first truly famous barman at the Savoy Hotel's American Bar in London, doing much to secure the bar's reputation. During her tenure there, from 1903 to 1924, Coleman invented many drinks, of which this was perhaps the most famous.

1 ½ oz. gin

1 ½ oz. sweet vermouth

2 dashes Fernet Branca (Campari, Angostura, or other bitters may be subsituted)

Combine ingredients in a cocktail shaker with cracked ice. Shake and strain into a chilled cocktail glass. Squeeze a bit of orange peel over the top. Do not stir, but let the orange essense float atop the drink.

FOR YOUR FURTHER DRINKING PLEASURE: On the other side of the Atlantic, a similar cocktail, the **Zaza**, made with equal parts gin and Dubonnet and no bitters at all, was wildly popular in the 1910s and 1920s and all but forgotten a few decades later. A slightly newer version of the Hanky Panky is the **Paddy**, dating from the 1930s. To make one, let Irish whiskey take the place of gin and omit the squeeze of orange peel.

Harlem

"I went for fifteen minutes and stayed three hours," said Babe Ruth of his first trip to the Cotton Club. Who could blame him? The Harlem hotspot boasted the best music in Manhattan, with Duke Ellington and Cab Calloway playing on alternate nights, Ethel Waters singing her showstopping "Stormy Weather," and a young unknown named Lena Horne making her debut in the chorus line. If you weren't there the night Calloway forgot the words to a song and covered the lapse by singing "hi-de-ho" — well, neither were we. But we can still imagine the moment as we sip the club's most popular cocktail.

2 – 3 chunks pineapple

½ tsp. maraschino liqueur

2 oz. gin

1 oz. pineapple juice

Place the pineapple chunks in a cocktail shaker, add the maraschino liqueur and crush lightly with a muddler. Add cracked ice, gin, and pineapple juice. Shake, strain into a chilled cocktail glass, and garnish with a maraschino cherry.

FOR YOUR FURTHER DRINKING PLEASURE: With a change of spirits, this drink becomes the venerable **Havana Special.** To make one, replace the gin with light rum, then double the amounts of pineapple juice and maraschino liqueur. Shake with ice and strain into a glass half-filled with crushed ice.

McClures

August

25 Cents

Honeymoon Cocktail

Early versions of this drink, which originated at Hollywood's Brown Derby restaurant in the early 1930s, called for equal parts apple brandy and Benedictine. It wasn't long, however, until the amount of brandy was increased and the Benedictine reduced — a wise decision, in our opinion.

1 ½ oz. calvados
½ oz. Benedictine
½ oz. orange curaçao
Juice of ½ lemon, strained

Combine ingredients in a cocktail shaker with cracked ice. Shake and strain into a chilled cocktail glass. Garnish with a twist of lemon peel.

FOR YOUR FURTHER DRINKING PLEASURE: For those who just can't get enough of the British monarchy, we offer **Princess Mary's Pride**, created by maestro Harry Craddock in 1922 to commemorate the wedding of one obscure royal (Princess Mary, aunt of the future Queen Elizabeth II) to another obscure royal. To create the libation, eliminate the lemon juice and replace the Benedictine and curaçao with ¾ ounce each of dry vermoth and Dubonnet.

Honolulu Cocktail

In its prime, Hollywood's famous Brown Derby gave rise to many signature comestibles, including Cobb salad, grapefruit cake (reportedly the favorite dessert of Joanne Woodward), and this refreshing cocktail, one of the first to cash in on the lure of the tropics and exotic new ingredients. Like canned pineapple juice, this drink debuted in the 1930s.

General Sherwood: How do you like your brandy, sir?
Philip Marlowe: In a glass.

— Charles Waldron and Humphrey Bogart in *The Big Sleep*, 1946

2 oz. gin
½ oz. pineapple juice
½ oz. orange juice
Juice of ¼ lemon, strained
Dash of Angostura bitters

Combine ingredients in a cocktail shaker with cracked ice. Shake and strain into a chilled cocktail glass. Garnish with a twist of lemon peel. For a showier drink, serve in a glass with a sugared rim. Although this is a modern flourish, the spirit of the drink remains authentic, as some early recipes called for the addition of a spoonful of powdered sugar.

Hot Buttered Rum

There are many recipes for hot buttered rum. The mix of spices is very much up to whoever is making the drinks, and mixologists develop their own favorite blends. This one comes to us from *The Gentleman's Companion*, which describes the recipe's originator as a seasoned sailor "best remembered for his tattooed masterpieces, haunch, paunch, and his Hot Buttered Rum." Remember to use heatproof glasses and mugs for all hot drinks.

1 tsp. brown sugar

1 tsp. fresh lemon juice, strained

1 twist lemon peel

4 – 6 whole cloves

2 oz. dark rum

Boiling water

1 tsp. butter

Place all ingredients except rum, water, and butter in a mug. Add rum, then boiling water. Float the butter on top, and drink when the butter has completely melted.

Hot Toddy

efore the advent of plentiful and inexpensive ice, hot cocktails were the drink of the day. In an age when the climate was unusually cold, heating was primitive, and outdoor work and travel unavoidable, hot drinks warmed as well as soothed. They were also the over-the-counter remedies of the day, taken for colds, sore throats, aches, and other complaints. Of the many drinks of this sort, the Hot Toddy is perhaps the best known, and one of the few to survive into our modern era of iced cocktails. A Hot Toddy can be made with many types of liquor, including whiskey, rum, Southern Comfort, brandy, and even gin and vodka, and the additive varied to complement the spirit used. Remember to use heatproof glasses and mugs for all hot drinks.

1 tsp. sugar

2 pinches ground cinnamon

1 pinch ground cloves

Slice of lemon

2 oz. whiskey, brandy, or rum

Boiling water

Place spices and lemon slice in a mug, then pour in whiskey Add boiling water and garnish with a cinnamon stick and a pinch of nutmeg.

Jack Rose

Yes, the drink does have a faintly rosie hue — but it also owes its name to Jack Rose, a colorful, if now forgotten, gangster of the 1920s.

2 oz. calvados or applejack

Juice of ⅓ lemon, strained

4 dashes grenadine

Combine ingredients in a cocktail shaker with cracked ice. Shake and strain into a chilled cocktail glass.

Jean Harlow

he silent era of film gave us sweet leading ladies with pansy eyes and long curling tresses. With sound came a new kind of starlet, red-lipped, silvery, and dangerous. Jean Harlow was the first of the platinum blondes, the woman for whom the epithet "blond bombshell" was created. Her aura lives on in this cocktail, as sexy and seductive as Harlow herself.

1 ½ oz. rum

1 ½ sweet vermouth

Pour rum and vermouth over ice in a cocktail shaker. Shake and strain into a chilled cocktail glass and garnish with a wedge of lemon.

FOR YOUR FURTHER DRINKING PLEASURE: Contemporary aficionados may be familiar with a cocktail called a **Gypsy**, which mixes vodka and Benedictine in a one-to-one ratio and adds a dash of bitters. This is a later version of the original Gypsy, which followed the proportions of the Jean Harlow but used gin rather than rum. If you make a gin Gypsy, do not shake, but stir with ice in a mixing glass and strain into a cocktail glass. To garnish, add a maraschino cherry.

There's pleasure in the offing when the drinks are to be made with Kentucky Tavern, a fine liquor of rare taste and quality that for over 73 years has been the stewardship of the same family.

Glenmore Distilleries Company, *Incorporated*, Louisville, Ky.

THERE'S ONLY ONE BETTER BUY IN BONDS...*WAR BONDS.*

Leap Year

Dry America's loss was Europe's gain. When Prohibition went into effect in 1920, barman Harry Craddock crossed the Atlantic and found work at London's Savoy Hotel. Five years later, he was head barman at the hotel's American Bar, where he remained in charge for the next fourteen years. Craddock was one of history's great mixologists, precise and inventive, and the creator of dozens of drinks. This one was whipped up for February 29, 1928 — leap year day. According to *The Savoy Cocktail Book*, it "was responsible for more proposals than any other cocktail that has ever been mixed." On your marks, get set, go!

2 oz. gin

1 tbsp. dry vermouth

1 tbsp. orange liqueur

Dash of fresh lemon juice

Dash of grenadine

Pour ingredients over ice in a cocktail shaker. Shake and strain into a chilled cocktail glass. Squeeze a piece of lemon peel over the top.

FOR YOUR FURTHER DRINKING PLEASURE: Similar to the Leap Year is another 1920s-era cocktail called the **Maiden's Blush**, which contains the same ingredients in the same proportions but eliminates the vermouth. We are also reminded of another, somewhat older British cocktail, the **Webster**. It uses the same amounts of gin and vermouth, but adds apricot brandy instead of orange liqueur, and a single dash of lime juice in place of lemon and grenadine. We don't know who Webster was, but we have it on good authority that his cocktail was extremely popular at the bar of the Cunard luxury liner *Mauretania*, and definitely the thing to have as one sped across the Atlantic in style.

Marlene Dietrich

In 1930, one day after *The Blue Angel* premiered in Germany, Marlene Dietrich left for the United States, never to return to her native country. The German actress instantly became one of Hollywood's most celebrated stars. This drink, named in her honor, originated at the Hi Ho Club. Whether it was a favorite cocktail of the star herself or whether it got its name because it mirrored Dietrich's blend of toughness and sexuality, we haven't been able to discover. Whatever the inspiration, it's well worth trying when you're looking for something with sweet top notes — and a swift undercurrent.

2 oz. rye

½ oz. orange curaçao

3 dashes Angostura bitters

1 wedge lemon

1 wedge orange

Pour rye, curaçao, and bitters into a shaker over cracked ice. Squeeze in lemon and orange wedges and discard the fruit. Shake briskly and strain into an old-fashioned glass filled with ice. A garnish of lemon or orange wedge is optional.

Mary Pickford

When your favorite before-dinner drink loses its appeal, try this apéritif for a refreshing change of pace.

1 ½ oz. light rum
1 ½ oz. pineapple juice
1 tsp. grenadine

Pour ingredients into a cocktail shaker over cracked ice. Shake briskly, strain into a chilled glass, and garnish with a spear of fresh pineapple.

FOR YOUR FURTHER DRINKING PLEASURE: Equally delightful is the **Silent Third**, still drunk in Europe, where it originated, but relatively undiscovered in America. To make one, increase the amount of rum to 2 ounces, omit the grenadine, and replace the pineapple juice with 1 ounce each of Cointreau and fresh lemon juice. Garnish with a twist of lemon peel.

Monkey Gland

Despite its curious name, this cock-tail has impeccable bloodlines, having been created at Harry's Bar in Paris. Who came up with the moniker remains a mystery. All we can say is, that's what happens when you let the customers name the cocktails — especially if they've already had a few of them.

Our studies reveal that classic European recipes call for Pernod, while American recipes of classic vintage tend to favor Benedictine.

2 oz. gin

1 oz. orange juice

3 dashes grenadine

3 dashes Pernod or Benedictine

Pour ingredients into a cocktail shaker over cracked ice. Shake and strain into a chilled glass.

FOR YOUR FURTHER DRINKING PLEASURE: The Monkey Gland is a racier version of an earlier staple of the Prohibition era, the **Orange Blossom**, which was straight-forward gin and orange juice without the fillip of either grenadine or Pernod. If good gin was available, the cocktail was mixed in a ratio of two parts gin to 1 part orange juice. If the gin was terrible, a half-and-half mix was employed. Then there is the **Colonial** cocktail, which is an Orange Blossom made with grape-fruit juice rather than orange, then enhanced with ½ ounce of maraschino liqueur and garnished with a cherry.

WHEN IN PARIS,
SAY SANK ROO DOE NOO

During Prohibition, 5 Rue Daunou glimmered for Americans like a mirage dancing on the desert. It was the Paris address of Harry's Bar (or Harry's New York Bar, if you want to be formal). Americans felt right at home there, surrounded by paneled walls shipped directly from New York, and felt

pennants emblazoned with the names of better-known American universities. If that didn't do the trick, the bar offered American hot dogs, the first ever served in France. All the Lost Generation drank at Harry's, and sometimes quarreled stupendously. One night Ernest Hemingway showed the door to a lion (the pet of a local pugilist) who had relieved himself on the writer's shoes. The creative spirit of the place was Harry MacElhone, formerly of Ciro's in London. Among the cocktails said to have been authored by MacElhone are the French 75, the Red Snapper, the Scofflaw, the Sidecar, and the White Lady. Although MacElhone passed away in 1958, his bar is still there to welcome Americans, especially on election nights, when expats are in a mood to squabble among themselves over this candidate or that. Whenever we're in Paris, we find ourselves following the advice in a Harry's ad that ran throughout the 1920s and 1930s — we ask our kindly taxi driver to deliver us to "Sank Roo Doe Noo."

The New 1920 Cocktail

n elaborate version of the classic Manhattan, with a lovely orange glow. This one is well worth reviving.

1 ½ oz. rye
¾ oz. dry vermouth
¾ oz. sweet vermouth
Dash of orange bitters

Pour ingredients over ice in a mixing glass. Stir well and strain into a chilled cocktail glass. Finish by squeezing a piece of lemon peel over the top.

FOR YOUR FURTHER DRINKING PLEASURE: A simple change of spirits — from rye to brandy — and the use of 2 dashes of Cointreau in place of orange bitters will give you one of the more delightful versions of a **Bombay** cocktail. The "new" cocktail of 1920 also reminds us of one of the oldest of vodka libations drunk in America, the **Czarina**, which substitutes vodka for rye and replaces the orange bitters with 1 ounce apricot brandy.

LIFE IN 1920

- Newly on the market: Chanel No. 5 perfume, pogo sticks, Baby Ruth bars.
- Newly off the market: booze — Prohibition began at midnight, January 6.
- New way of getting around the law: Gentlemen stash their alcohol in hollow walking canes, ladies secure flasks under their silk garters.
- New item to buy: a portable still, sold at local hardware stores for $6.
- Newlyweds Mary Pickford and Douglas Fairbanks make their home, Pickfair, Hollywood's first grand mansion.
- Newlyweds on the opposite coast, Scott and Zelda Fitzgerald, cavort in the fountain of the Plaza Hotel and ride down the avenues on taxicab roofs.

Oriental

Part of the art of mixology is having an enticing story to go with each and every drink. One of the all-time greats, Harry Craddock of London's Savoy Hotel, frequently made notes on the drinks he served. Whether this story is true or not we cannot be certain — but we like to think it is. According to Craddock, an American engineer working in the Philippines in 1924 became deathly ill. He survived a long bout of fever only through the faithful ministrations of his doctor. After making a full recovery, he searched for something valuable enough to repay his debt of gratitude. Eventually, he parted with the recipe for this cocktail. As far as we know, the doctor was more than satisfied with the tribute.

This cocktail works best with straight rye (whiskey that is predominantly rye) rather then the blended ryes more common today.

2 oz. straight rye
1 oz. dry vermouth
1 oz. orange curaçao
Juice of ½ lime, strained

Pour ingredients into a cocktail shaker over cracked ice. Shake and strain into a chilled glass.

Papa Doble

During the 1940s and 1950s, when Ernest Hemingway lived in a villa near Havana, he was such a frequent patron at El Floridita that a corner barstool was perpetually reserved for him. A man who knew his way around a bar, Hemingway concocted his own *grande* version of the humble daiquiri. For the larger-than-life writer, this recipe served one — himself. We lesser mortals should look for a friend to share it with, as the volume of rum packs the wallop of a tropical gale.

Contemporary recipes often call for grenadine rather than maraschino liqueur, and add a maraschino cherry garnish. Well, if you must — but we cringe to think what Hemingway would say to this.

It's funny what a wonderful gentility you get in the bar of a big hotel.

– Ernest Hemingway, *The Sun Also Rises*, 1926

3 oz. plus 1 ½ tbsp. white rum, preferably Bacardi
Juice of 2 limes, strained
Juice of ½ grapefruit, strained
6 drops maraschino liqueur

Place 1 generous cup cracked ice in a blender. Add all ingredients and blend on high just until the mixture turns cloudy. Pour into two cocktail glasses and drink at once.

Parkeroo

It took Americans quite a while to figure out what, exactly, to do with tequila. As late as 1956, the otherwise comprehensive *Esquire Drink Book* offered just three recipes using the liquor, and felt it necessary to describe to readers the local custom of taking shots with salt and a wedge of lemon. The Parkeroo, as documented by Lucius Beebe in *The Stork Club Bar Book*, is one of the earliest attempts by a private citizen to make use of the stuff. We offer it in tribute to man's sense of adventure and because the inventor's commentary, below, is worth preserving for the ages.

While painting a picket fence around my house . . .
I discovered that after two Parkeroos I could remain stationary
and let the fence revolve around the brush.

– Lucius Beebe, *The Stork Club Bar Book*, 1930

1 oz. tequila
2 oz. dry sherry

Pour ingredients over shaved ice in a mixing glass. Allow to chill for a few moments, then strain into a chilled cocktail glass. Garnish with a twist of lemon peel.

Planter's Punch

There's no dodging the fact that we must expect to use decent rum. This recently born swarm of new, strange rums can no more replace even a fair Jamaica, Barbados, or Haitian rum than Mr. Kreisler can play the E Flat Nocturne on a turnip crate.

— Charles Baker, Jr. , *The Gentleman's Companion*, 1939

There are innumerable recipes for this cocktail, which was drunk throughout the coastal Southern states and the Caribbean. We offer two of our favorites, the first because it is simple and delicious, the second because it's a fine example of versions that incorporate more exotic ingredients, yet resists the temptation to become too cluttered. One thing that we have noticed is common to all versions is the large amount of alcohol used, making them twice — and sometimes even thrice — the strength of a standard cocktail. We advise sharing with a friend and sipping slowly — preferably on a veranda that is not too far off the ground.

JAMAICAN STYLE

4 oz. aged Jamaican rum

Juice of 1 lime, strained

2 tsp. superfine sugar

Combine ingredients in a mixing glass and stir until sugar is completely dissolved. Pack a chilled old fashioned glass with shaved or finely crushed ice and pour ingredients over the ice. Garnish with a slice of orange, a spear of pineapple, and fresh mint.

SAVANNAH STYLE

2 oz. aged Jamaican rum

3 oz. cognac

Juice of 1 lime or ½ lemon, strained

¾ oz. chilled pineapple juice

Combine ingredients in a mixing glass and stir. Pack a tall, chilled glass with shaved or finely crushed ice and pour ingredients over the ice. Garnish with a wedge of orange, a spear of pineapple, and a maraschino cherry.

Punches

Until the cocktail came along, punch was the festive libation of choice, a step up from everyday ales and wines. American colonists brought a taste for punches with them from Europe, but that taste had itself been imported into Europe from Asia. The word punch is said to come from the Hindi *pancha*, for "five," the number of ingredients to be used. Unlike the ales and wines of the day, punches were exotic and fanciful. Modest concoctions might be mostly wine, but hosts who wanted to show off the plentitude of their households or social clubs were sure to incorporate expensive ingredients like rum, spices, oranges, pineapple, and other fresh fruits. Following are some of our favorite punches, and tips for making them.

(If you've come to this page looking for Planter's Punch, it's time to brush up your knowledge index. Planter's Punch isn't considered a punch per se but a cocktail, and you'll find the recipe on page 64.)

Rules for Making Perfect Punch

- Use fresh, rather than canned or frozen fruits whenever possible.
- Chill all ingredients — liquors, juices, sodas, and fruits — at least two hours in advance, and preferably longer.
- Combine liquors the night before you serve the punch. This gives the flavors a chance to mingle and mellow.
- Add sparkling wines and sodas just as your guests arrive.

🍸 Use a large block of ice rather than ice cubes in your punch bowl. Large ice melts much more slowly and won't dilute your punch.

🍸 Don't make too much punch at a time, as sparkling wines and carbonated sodas go flat quickly.

🍸 Don't get lazy. As the first batch is drunk, there's a tendency to start dumping ingredients in willy-nilly. Mix the last bowl as carefully as you mixed the first.

BENGAL LANCERS PUNCH

From the exotic East, where punch began, comes a delicate and elegant punch that summons the ruby tint of sunset on distant shores.

4 c. red bordeaux wine

3 oz. light rum

3 oz. orange liqueur

½ c. orange juice

½ c. pineapple juice

Juice of 4–6 limes (enough to make ½ c.), strained

4 c. club soda

4 c. champagne

Follow the directions for making perfect punch (above), taking care to add the club soda and champagne just before drinking. Float thin slices of lime in the punch bowl as a garnish.

FISH HOUSE PUNCH

The oldest and best known of all American punches was invented by the happy anglers of the Fish House Club of Philadelphia, who enjoyed rounding off a day's fishing with an evening of eating and drinking. According to legend, the recipe remained a secret for almost two hundred years, then surfaced at the beginning of the twentieth century. This is how it appeared in 1934, in Patrick Gavin Duffy's *Official Mixer's Manual* and, except for the substitution of club soda for spring water, as close to the 1734 original as one is likely to get. This may seem like quite a lot of sugar to the contemporary palate. We advise starting with half this much, then sweetening to taste.

1 c. brandy

½ c. peach brandy

½ c. dark rum

Juice of 6 lemons, strained

½ lb. powdered sugar

12 c. club soda

Follow the directions for making perfect punch (pages 66–67), but stir sugar into a tumbler of club soda to dissolve it before adding it to the punch bowl.

KIRSCHWASSER PUNCH

Kirschwasser, a type of cherry brandy, is an excellent punch bowl choice, as it brings out other flavors. This recipe, adapted from *The Gentleman's Companion*, notes that the amount of maraschino liqueur should never be more than one third of the amount of kirschwasser, and in some recipes the former is left out altogether.

As with Fish House Punch, opposite, we caution you to start with a small amount of sugar, then sweeten to taste.

1 ½ c. kirschwasser
½ c. (or less) maraschino liqueur
4 c. Rhine or Sauterne wine
4 c. pineapple juice
½ lb. (about 1 c., or less)
superfine sugar
2 c. club soda
Fresh pineapple
Fresh grapefruit

Follow the directions for making perfect punch (pages 66-67), but stir sugar into a tumbler of club soda to dissolve it before adding to the punch bowl. Float chunks of fresh pineapple and segments of grapefruit in the bowl.

Rasputin

What's a bon vivant to do? Appalled by the ravages of temperance, Charles Baker Jr. set off from his native shores in search of conviviality and thrilling new cocktails. His quest resulted in *The Gentleman's Companion* and *The South American* *Gentleman's Companion* — volumes worth the consideration of any serious sophisticate. This libation, which Baker discovered at the Chateau Caucasien in Buenos Aires, makes use of an ingredient virtually unknown in America at the time — vodka.

Why they elected to name it after that sticky mad monk was not disclosed.
– Charles Baker Jr., *The South American Gentleman's Companion*, 1939

2 oz. best-quality vodka
1 ½ oz. cassis syrup
½ – 1 tsp. Rose's lime juice, depending on your taste

Combine ingredients in a cocktail shaker with cracked ice. Shake and strain into a chilled cocktail glass

FOR YOUR FURTHER DRINKING PLEASURE: Similar to the Rasputin is another vodka classic, popular during that era when Russian aristocrats exiled by the Revolution found themselves making the best of it in Paris. **The Ballet Russe** begins like the Rasputin with 2 ounces vodka, reduces the amount of cassis syrup to a mere tablespoon, and uses fresh lime juice in place of Rose's.

Ron Habañero-Dubonnet Helado

This cocktail, which comes to us by way of *The South American Gentleman's Companion*, by Charles Baker Jr., is one of the more unusual recipes we came across, and an interesting change of pace from the ubiquitous frozen daiquiri. According to Baker, it was created at the Café Plaza in Maracaibo, Venezuela.

Baker doesn't specify whether Dubonnet red or white is required. We suspect he used the red version, as he references the cocktail's rosy hue. We cannot be sure, since white Dubonnet is also a frequent pairing with rum, and the grenadine would, on its own, add a somewhat rosy tint. You may also wish to try golden or dark rum instead of white, which results in a somewhat bolder-tasting cocktail. If you don't care for blended drinks, not to worry — this one can be shaken and poured, ice and all, into a chilled cocktail glass.

1 ½ oz. white rum

1 oz. Dubonnet

1 tsp. grenadine

1 tsp. fresh lime juice, strained

Place ingredients in a blender with a handful of cracked ice. Whir just until blended, then pour into a frosted cocktail glass.

*R*ose

This satin slipper of a drink was invented by Johnny Mitta, bartender at the Chatham Hotel in Paris, in 1922. The Chatham was in prime drinking territory, not far from Harry's New York Bar, and cocktail enthusiasts were soon clamoring for the libation wherever they went. If you spend your time poring over old cocktail books as we do, you will notice that in American recipes the syrup called for is almost always grenadine or raspberry — a fallback position, as the red currant syrup used in the original was unavailable this side of the Atlantic. Thanks to the recent popularity of flavored syrups, we're happy to report that the missing ingredient can now be obtained, and the drink can be authentically replicated. Sip it and hark back to those moveable feast days when *le jazz* was hot and modernism was oh so *moderne*.

2 oz. dry vermouth

1 oz. cherry brandy

1 tsp. red currant syrup

Stir ingredients in a mixing glass with cracked ice, then strain into a chilled cocktail glass. **FOR YOUR FURTHER DRINKING PLEASURE**: There is another, somewhat anglicized version of this drink you should also be aware of, one we'll call an **English Rose** for clarification. In this version, the ingredients consist of ¾ oz. dry vermouth, ¾ oz. cherry or apricot brandy, and 1 ½ oz. gin. The currant syrup is replaced by grenadine or, in some recipes, left out altogther.

Royal

The Royal was a favorite at Hollywood's Embassy Club, which on any given night held more stars per square inch than any spot on earth.

Think of this as a pared-down version of a Singapore Sling — sleek and sophisticated, as befits old-time Hollywood.

1 ½ oz. gin
¾ oz. dry vermouth
¾ oz. cherry brandy

Pour ingredients into a mixing glass filled with ice. Stir, strain into a chilled cocktail glass, and garnish with a twist of lemon.

FOR YOUR FURTHER DRINKING PLEASURE: If you miss the zip and fizz of a Singapore Sling, oh, do we have a drink for you. The long-neglected **Desert Healer** combines the virtues of the Singapore Sling and the immortal Screwdriver. To make one, follow the proportions above but replace the vermouth with 1 ½ ounces chilled orange juice. Stir in a mixing glass with ice, strain into a tall glass with three or four ice cubes, fill to the rim with ginger ale, and garnish with a wheel of orange and a cherry. We're not sure where this drink got its name, but it's definitely worth wandering in the desert for. Another drink of this type was the **White Lady**, a popular drink of the Roaring Twenties, which calls for the same proportions as the Royal but uses Cointreau and fresh lemon juice in place of the vermouth and brandy.

Rusty Nail

Pity the poor Rusty Nail, a noble drink that seldom gets the respect it deserves. Contemporary aficionados are wont to dismiss it as a concoction of the 1950s, and scoff at the notion that a true Scot would tolerate the incestuous blending of scotch and Drambuie. Like Formica and the shopping mall, it is seen as an unfortunate token of postwar American excess. There is one point on which we are in complete agreement with these pundits – made to their specifications, with ingredients brutishly blended, the drink is indeed a travesty. A little research, however, shows that the Rusty Nail is far older than generally asserted. A recipe appears as early as 1930, in *The Savoy Cocktail Book*. We follow their proportions for the drink on the opposite page, and are indebted to them for a cleaner method of mixing, which yields a better drink than later recipes.

Nora: I got rid of all those reporters.
Nick: What did you tell them?
Nora: We're out of scotch.
Nick: What a gruesome idea.

— William Powell and Myrna Loy in *Another Thin Man*, 1939

1 ½ oz. scotch

1 tbsp. Drambuie

Place several ice cubes in an old fashioned glass. Pour scotch over the ice, then float the Drambuie on top. Do not stir, but let the ingredients mingle at their own rate in the icy chill.

FOR YOUR FURTHER DRINKING PLEASURE: The Rusty Nail is a more elaborate version of the equally elegant **Scotch Mist**. No mixing per se is needed for a Scotch Mist, and the drink's success hinges on having a quantity of shaved ice on hand. To create, fill an old fashioned glass with shaved ice, pour your favorite scotch over the ice, and add a twist of lemon peel. A slightly lighter scotch classic is the post-WWII **Stone Fence**, not to be confused with the prewar drink of the same name, which was made with cider and whiskey or calvados (apple brandy). The Stone Fence of the 1950s begins with several cubes of ice in a tall glass. Pour 1 ½ ounces scotch over the ice, add a dash of Angostura bitters, and fill to the top with club soda. How this smooth drink got its rough name we aren't sure — we climbed over several of them with no problem at all!

WWII:
THE SECOND
PROHIBITION

One reason people are so likely to assume that scotch drinks originated in the 1950s may be because they were so popular during that decade. Few things summarize the mortgaged-up and but-toned-down era of country clubs, tail fins, and patios as well as a glass of scotch on the rocks. Even at the time, scotch had an iconlike status, a sign that the back-to-back eras of Prohibition, Depression, and global conflagration were finally at an end. For drinkers, it had been a rough half-century. No sooner had Prohibition been repealed than war came along to create a second round of scarcity. Alcohol was a key ingredient in explosives, and American distillers voluntarily converted 100 percent of their production to war work. They figured the four-year surplus of whiskey in their inventories would carry them through the crisis. What they forgot to take into account was that a nation under stress and on the move is prone to drink more. America's alcohol consumption leapt from 140 million gallons per year on the eve of the war to 190 million gallons in 1942. It wasn't long until the inventories were gone. Though rationing still technically allowed adults to purchase a fifth of as Aqua Velva mixed with cola or grapefruit juice made a palatable cocktail, as did alcohol from the infirmary mixed with torpedo fluid.   In the wildly popular WWII story *Mister Roberts*, one of the crew, Ensign Pulver, has lured a nurse into a date by promising her a drink of real scotch. With the aid of Roberts and the ship's doctor, he concocts a potion that looks and tastes vaguely like Johnny Walker Red Label. Into the mix go rub-

Let's go to a phone booth or something, huh? Where I will unveil a fifth of whiskey I have hidden under my loose, flowing sports shirt.

– Frank Sinatra woos Donna Reed in
From Here to Eternity, 1953

whiskey a month, the scarcity of goods made the coupons all but useless. By 1944, there was no liquor at all on the shelves, and people began to look back on Prohibition as a kind of golden age. Times were just as dry for soldiers overseas. Announcement of the arrival of a new shipment of aftershave sent a current of excitement through many a camp, bing alcohol, Coca-Cola, a few drops of iodine, and finally, for aging, a bit of coal-tar-based hair tonic. The scene in the play, and later the movie, inevitably got a large and knowing laugh from ex-servicemen. Is it any wonder that real scotch, plentiful and affordable once again, became a signature drink of the 1950s?

Sangrita

Sangria, ubiquitous in Mexican restaurants as far north as the Bering Straits, seemed to burst on the American bar scene with such force that at one time we suspected it had been a mass import effort by college students returning from spring break. Actually, one can find recipes for single-glass wine cocktails dating back to the 1930s. Like sangria punches, Sangrita is a free-form cocktail, and variations are the rule rather than the exception. This version, which Lucius Beebe collected for *The Stork Club Bar Book*, was reputed to be a favorite of Mexico's brave matadors.

2 oz. red bordeaux wine
½ oz. pineapple juice
Juice of 1 small lime, strained
Club soda

Pour wine and fruit juices over ice in a tall collins glass. Stir, then fill to the top with club soda. Garnish with a wedge of lime or a few chunks of pineapple.

Satan's Whiskers

We admit that this drink appeals not only to our palate but to the show-off lurking within. According to Harry Craddock's *The Savoy Cocktail Book*, first published in 1930 and still one of the first authorities we turn to, there are two versions of this drink. Depending on which variety of orange liqueur you prefer, Satan's Whiskers are either curled or straight — curled if made with the slightly lighter-tasting orange curaçao, straight if made with Grand Marnier. Whichever way our whims run, we take great comfort in a mixologist who understands our order, and settle in for a cozy night at the bar.

¾ oz. gin

¾ oz. dry vermouth

¾ oz. sweet vermouth

¾ oz. orange juice

2 tsp. orange liqueur: curaçao for a cocktail with curled whiskers,

Grand Marnier for a libation with straight whiskers

Dash of orange bitters

Combine ingredients in a cocktail shaker with cracked ice. Shake and strain into a chilled cocktail glass. Garnish with a twist of orange peel. If you do not have orange bitters on hand, Angostura is an acceptable substitute.

Savoy Tango

amed for the bar at London's Savoy Hotel, where it was invented, this cocktail summons up the smokey, sexy side of the 1920s. The tango, that outrageously torrid dance of the gauchos, reached New York in the winter of 1910–11. A decade later, Rudolph Valentino tangoed with Alice Terry in *The Four Horsemen of the Apocalypse* and the dance became an international sensation. Although we cannot be certain what year this cocktail made its debut, the mixologists at the Savoy's American Bar were ever on the cutting edge, and our guess is that it premiered soon after Valentino did his smoldering dance on the silver screen.

1 ½ oz. sloe gin

1 ½ oz. calvados

Pour ingredients into a cocktail shaker over cracked ice.

Shake and strain into a chilled cocktail glass.

FOR YOUR FURTHER DRINKING PLEASURE: Very similar to the Savoy Tango is the **Ping-Pong**, which is made exactly like the Tango, but uses crème de violette instead of Calvados. Because crème de violette was more popular in Europe than in America, it is likely that this cocktail originated there, probably in the 1920s, when the game of Ping-Pong was enjoying a resurgence of popularity. An American drink book of the same period, *The Old Waldorf-Astoria Bar Book*, gives a recipe for a Ping-Pong that uses equal parts sloe gin and dry vermouth, and adds a dash of orange bitters. If you've an urge to try the European version of the drink, Parfait Amour is an acceptable substitute for the very hard to find crème de violette.

A VERY BIG DEAL:
THE COCKTAIL SHAKER

The truth is, in a pinch you can shake or mix a drink in an old peanut butter jar.

So why are cocktail shakers such a big deal? Why, at the mere mention of the word, do our minds fill with visions of chrome deco masterpieces of the 1930s?

Special cups and containers for mixing both alcoholic and nonalcoholic drinks go far back in time. The ancient Egyptians had them, as did South Americans. The modern cocktail shaker got its start in the 1880s, when a bartender discovered that instead of mixing drinks by pouring the ingredients back and forth between two glasses, he could fit the mouth of a smaller glass snugly into the mouth of a larger glass and shake the contents "with a bit of show" that pleased his customers.

Of course, everybody wanted to repeat the maneuver at home, and soon mass-produced shakers were appearing on the market. There was something to suit everyone's pocketbook — silver for the well-heeled, glass or nickel-plated for the common man. Metal, by the way, chills faster and stays cold longer than glass does and, all other things being equal, is almost always a better choice.

Prohibition, that long and grim experiment, was only a minor setback for the cocktail shaker. When Prohibition ended, the shaker became an instant icon, a symbol of the new freedom and, with the Depression still raging, hope for a return to the prosperity of old. Movies that sought to establish the wit, sophistication, and affluence of the main characters showed them with shaker in hand, mixing, pouring, and quipping away. Films like *The Thin Man*, *My Man Godfrey*, *The Gay Divorcee*, *Topper*, *The Philadelphia Story* and dozens of others made no bones about glamorizing drinking as a refined pastime of the upper classes. The classic chrome shaker was on display in frame after frame, shouting the end of Prohibition and burning its way into the American psyche. To this day, except for brief flirtations with kitschy glass shakers in the 1950s and '60s, the deco-designed metal cylinder remains the shaker of choice, well designed and perfectly suited to the task.

South Side

Contrary to the somewhat misleading name, this Prohibition-era cocktail hails from New York, not Chicago. It earned its fame at that most flagrant and elegant of speakeasies, "21" — referred to as "the numbers" by those in the know. Prohibition agents frequently set their sights on the club, where celebrities and the well-heeled drank with abandon, yet owners Jack Kriendler and Charlie Berns always managed to evade the law. Knowing what they were up against, they'd installed an elaborate system of pulleys and levers that, within moments of being deployed, swept every bottle from the shelves and bar and dumped the shattered mess down a chute connected to the city sewer system. When the danger passed, the bar was resupplied from an equally ingenious secret wine cellar. Located not at "21" but next door at 19 West 52nd Street, the cache was protected by a two-ton door that could be opened only by inserting a meat skewer in a nearly invisible hole in one of many bricks in a whole wall of equally worn and pockmarked bricks. We never sip a South Side without toasting Prohibition, which brought out the genius and creativity of so many Americans.

1 ½ oz. gin

2 – 3 tsp. powdered sugar

Juice of 1 lemon, strained

Chilled club soda

2 sprigs fresh mint

Combine gin, powdered sugar, and lemon juice in a cocktail shaker with ice. Place two ice cubes in a highball glass and strain the contents of the shaker into the glass. Fill with club soda and garnish with mint sprigs.

Stork Club

olumnist Walter Winchell called it "the New Yorkiest spot in New York" and made it his adjunct office. In an era when nightclubs reigned supreme, the Stork Club had neither floor show nor orchestra. It didn't even have a jazz combo or a girl singer. Yet the nightly show — a parade of movie stars, Broadway babies, millionaires, and moguls – was so alluring that crowds gathered just to watch the arrivals and departures. Is it any wonder that the place soon had a cocktail named after it?

Of all the gin joints of all the towns in the world, she walks into mine!

— Humphrey Bogart yearns for Ingrid Bergman in *Casablanca*, 1943

1 ½ oz. gin
½ oz. triple sec
Juice of ½ lime, strained
1 oz. orange juice
Dash of Angostura bitters

Combine ingredients in a cocktail shaker with cracked ice. Shake and strain into a chilled cocktail glass. Garnish with a twist of lemon peel.

Tequila Special

This cocktail makes us bemoan the success of the Tequila Sunrise, for the Sunrise's massive popularity has dampened the prospects for all other tequila drinks out to make a name for themselves. This fine cooler, dating back to the 1930s, well deserves a revival.

2 oz. tequila

2 dashes orange bitters

Juice of 1 lime, strained

1 tsp. sugar

Club soda

Fill a tall glass two thirds full with ice. Add tequila, bitters, lime juice, sugar, and a few chunks cut from the squeezed lime. Stir to thoroughly dissolve sugar, then fill with club soda.

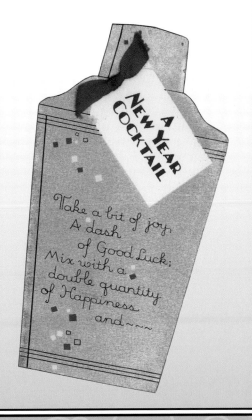

Tom and Jerry

Before the advent of plentiful and inexpensive ice, hot cocktails were the drink of the day. This one was the invention of "Professor" Jerry Thomas in the early 1850s, when he commanded the Planter's House Bar in St. Louis. Thomas, the first great American mixologist, was also an impressive merchandiser. He called his version of a hot toddy a Blue Blazer, because he set a match to the whiskey and mixed the drink by pouring the flaming blue mass from one tumbler to another. In New York, he refused to serve anyone a Tom and Jerry before the year's first snowfall, thus ensuring that it became a sought-after drink during the holiday season.

Remember to use heatproof glasses and mugs for all hot drinks.

1 egg, separated

1 tsp. sugar

1 oz. rum

1 oz. brandy

Optional spices: ground cinnamon, ground cloves, ground nutmeg

Boiling water

Beat the egg yolk until it is thin and ribbony. Beat the egg white until it is thick. Combine yolk and white, and transfer to a serving mug. Add sugar, rum, and brandy and stir gently. Add a pinch of spices, if desired. Fill mug with boiling water and garnish with a sprinkle of nutmeg.

UN **DUBONNET**

vin tonique au quinquina

Valencia

This delightful champagne cocktail was an international favorite. It cast its golden glow on Europe between the wars, and was a popular specialty of the house at the Roosevelt Hotel in Los Angeles. One sip and you'll understand why.

2 oz. apricot brandy

1 oz. chilled orange juice

4 dashes orange bitters

3 oz. ice cold champagne

Pour brandy, orange juice, and orange bitters into a cocktail shaker with cracked ice. Shake and strain into a chilled champagne flute or wineglass. Immediately top with cold champagne.

Ward 8

All politics is local. And, in some cases, so are all cocktails. In the early days of mixology, it was fashionable to create drinks commemorating community events and personalities. On election eve, 1884, a band of revelers at Boston's Locke-Ober Winter Palace Wine Rooms clamored for a drink to celebrate Martin M. Lomasney's impending victory in his run for the state legislature. The bartender dutifully honored their request and named the result after Lomasney's home district, Ward 8. The fact that this cocktail has survived its namesake as well as wars, Prohibition, and a century's worth of newer cocktails is proof of its eternal congeniality.

Take into consideration that the original version of this cocktail almost certainly used straight rye — whiskey that is predominantly rye, as opposed to the blended ryes of today. You may want to go to the trouble of procuring a bottle of straight rye, although many competent modern mixologists call for blended rye or even bourbon in their recipes.

1 ½ oz. rye

1 tsp. grenadine

¾ oz. chilled orange juice

Juice of ½ lemon, strained

Combine ingredients in a cocktail shaker with cracked ice. Shake and strain into a chilled cocktail glass. Garnish with a maraschino cherry and, depending on your predilection, a wedge of lemon or wheel of orange.

COCKTAILS LISTED BY MAIN SPIRIT

BRANDY
Blue Train Special
Bombay
Brandy Alexander
Corpse Reviver
Deauville
Depth Bomb
Embassy
English Rose
Fish House
 Punch
Rose
Valencia

BRANDY, CALVADOS
Honeymoon
Jack Rose
Princess Mary's
 Pride

BRANDY, COGNAC
Flying Fortress

CHAMPAGNE
Bengal Lancer's
 Punch
Champagne Fizz
Champagne Pick
 Me Up
Gloria Swanson

GIN
Alexander
Bronx
Bulldog
Clover Club
Clover Leaf

Colonial
Depth Charge
Desert Healer
Douglas Fairbanks
Gimlet
Gin & Tonic
Gold
Goldfish
Gypsy
Hanky Panky
Harlem
Honolulu
Leap Year
Maiden's Blush
Martini
Midnight
Minnehaha
Monkey Gland
Montauk
Orange Blossom
Queen's Cocktail
Royal
Satan's Whiskers
South Side
Stork Club
Tom Collins
Webster
White Lady
Zaza

GIN, SLOE
Futurity
Ping-Pong
Savoy Tango

RUM
Air Mail
Bee's Kiss
Brown Derby
 (variation)
Daiquiri
El Floridita
Floridita Daiquiri
Floridita Naturel
Havana Special
Hot Buttered Rum
Jean Harlow
Mai-Tai
Mary Pickford
Mulata
Papa Doble
Planter's Punch
Ron Collins
Ron Habañero-
 Dubonnet Helado
Silent Third
Tom and Jerry

SOUTHERN COMFORT
Scarlett O'Hara
Southern Collins

TEQUILA
Margarita
Parkeroo
Tequila Special
Tequila Sunrise

VODKA
Alexander the Great
Ballet Russe
Barbara

Bloody Mary
Czarina
Gypsy
Rasputin
Screwdriver

WHISKEY
Brown Derby
Gloom Lifter
Hot Toddy

WHISKY, IRISH
Paddy

WHISKEY, RYE
1920
Algonquin
Manhattan
Marlene Dietrich
Oriental
Scofflaw
Ward 8

WHISKEY, SCOTCH
Bobby Burns
Rusty Nail
Scotch Mist
Stone Fence

WINE
Kirschwasser Punch
Sangrita

INDEX